GW00602004

# Revise

## Maths and English

## KS1: YEAR 1

# Age 5–6

**Paul Broadbent, Peter Patilla and Louis Fidge**

## The *WHS Revise* series

The *WHS Revise* books enable you to help your child revise and practise important skills taught in school. These skills form part of the National Curriculum and will help your child to improve his or her Maths and English.

## Testing in schools

During their time at school all children will undergo a variety of tests. Regular testing is a feature of all schools. It is carried out:

● *informally* – in everyday classroom activities your child's teacher is continually assessing and observing your child's performance in a general way
● *formally* – more regular formal testing helps the teacher check your child's progress in specific areas.

Testing is important because:

● it provides evidence of your child's achievement and progress
● it helps the teacher decide which skills to focus on with your child
● it helps compare how different children are progressing.

## The importance of revision

Regular revision is important to ensure your child remembers and practises skills he or she has been taught. These books will help your child revise and test his or her knowledge of some of the things he or she will be expected to know. They will help you prepare your child to be in a better position to face tests in school with confidence.

## How to use this book

### Units

This book is divided into 28 units (14 for Maths and 14 for English), each focusing on one key skill. Each unit begins with a **Remember** section, which introduces and revises essential information about the particular skill covered. If possible, read and discuss this with your child to ensure he or she understands it.

This is followed by a **Have a go** section, which contains a number of activities to help your child revise the topic thoroughly and use the skill effectively. Usually, your child should be able to undertake these activities fairly independently.

### Revision tests

There are four revision tests in this book: two for Maths (pages 18–21) and two for English (pages 41–43). These test the skills covered in the preceding units and assess your child's progress and understanding. They can be marked by you or by your child. Your child should fill in his or her test score for each test in the space provided. This will provide a visual record of your child's progress and an instant sense of confidence and achievement.

### Parents' notes

The parents' notes (on pages 22–23 for Maths and pages 44–45 for English) provide you with brief information on each skill and explain why it is important.

### Answers

Answers to the unit questions and tests may be found on pages 24–26 for Maths and pages 46–48 for English.

First published 2007
exclusively for WHSmith by
Hodder Education, an Hachette UK Company,
338 Euston Road
London
NW1 3BH

Impression number   10 9 8 7 6 5 4 3 2
Year                2010  2009

Text and illustrations © Hodder Education 2007

All rights reserved. No part of this publication may be reproduced or transmitted in any form or by any means, electronic or mechanical, including photocopying, recording or any information storage and retrieval system, without permission in writing from the publisher.

A CIP record for this book is available from the British Library.

Cover illustration by Sally Newton Illustrations

Typeset by Fakenham Photosetting Limited, Fakenham, Norfolk

ISBN   978 034 094 2635

Printed and bound in Spain.

# Contents

# Unit 1: Reading and writing numbers

 **Remember**

The symbol **0** means **zero**, **nothing**, **nought**.

Numbers can be broken up into tens and ones.

| | | | |
|---|---|---|---|
| 10 = 10 + 0 | 13 = 10 + 3 | 16 = 10 + 6 | 19 = 10 + 9 |
| 11 = 10 + 1 | 14 = 10 + 4 | 17 = 10 + 7 | 20 = 20 + 0 |
| 12 = 10 + 2 | 15 = 10 + 5 | 18 = 10 + 8 | 21 = 20 + 1 |

 **Have a go**

**1** Write the missing numbers.

| | | | |
|---|---|---|---|
| a 12 = ☐ + 2 | b 15 = ☐ + 5 | c 17 = ☐ + 7 | d 19 = ☐ + 9 |
| e 11 = 10 + ☐ | f 13 = 10 + ☐ | g 16 = 10 + ☐ | h 18 = 10 + ☐ |

These are larger numbers:

| | | | |
|---|---|---|---|
| i 22 = ☐ + 2 | j 24 = ☐ + 4 | k 27 = ☐ + 7 | l 28 = ☐ + 8 |
| m 23 = 20 + ☐ | n 25 = 20 + ☐ | o 26 = 20 + ☐ | p 29 = 20 + ☐ |

**2** Join each number to its name.

twenty-four

twenty-one

fifteen

 12     21     30     25     15     14    24

fourteen

twenty-five

thirty

twelve

# Unit 2: Comparing numbers

## Remember

**Number lines** help you to compare numbers.

getting bigger →

← getting smaller

## Have a go

1 Look at the pairs of numbers. Colour the bigger number red.

   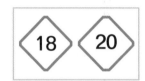

2 Look at the pairs of numbers. Colour the smaller number blue.

3 Fill in the numbers in between.

a 6 → ◯ ◯ ← 9      b 0 → ◯ ◯ ← 3

c 10 → ◯ ◯ ← 13    d 9 → ◯ ◯ ← 12

e 13 → ◯ ◯ ← 16    f 17 → ◯ ◯ ← 20

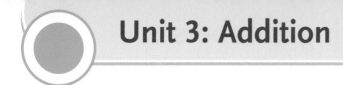

# Unit 3: Addition

## Remember

You can use a **number line** to help you add.

3 more than 2 equals 5

## Have a go

1 Write in the missing numbers.

| a | b | c |
|---|---|---|
| 3 more than 5 equals ☐ | 3 more than ☐ equals 6 | ☐ more than 4 equals 6 |
| 4 more than 2 equals ☐ | 2 more than ☐ equals 10 | ☐ more than 2 equals 5 |
| 5 more than 7 equals ☐ | 1 more than ☐ equals 8 | ☐ more than 6 equals 10 |
| 3 more than 8 equals ☐ | 4 more than ☐ equals 11 | ☐ more than 5 equals 8 |
| 2 more than 6 equals ☐ | 5 more than ☐ equals 9 | ☐ more than 9 equals 11 |

2 Answer these number sentences.

a Total 4 and 6 ⬭

b Add 5 to 6 ⬭

c 4 more than 3 ⬭

d Count on 3 from 5 ⬭

e 2 added to 9 ⬭

f Add together 2 and 5 ⬭

# Unit 4: Using doubles

## Remember

You can use **doubles** to help you add **near doubles**.

double 2

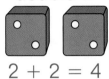

2 + 2 = 4

one more than double 2

2 + 3 = 5

## Have a go

**1** Add these doubles.

a 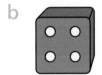  Total

b 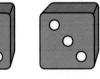 Total

c Total

d Total

e   Total

**2** Add these near doubles.

a   Total

b   Total

c Total

d Total

e   Total

## Remember

**Addition facts** that make 10 are important.

| 10 + 0<br>0 + 10 | 9 + 1<br>1 + 9 | 8 + 2<br>2 + 8 | 7 + 3<br>3 + 7 | 6 + 4<br>4 + 6 | 5 + 5 |

## Have a go

**1** Write in the missing numbers.

| a | b | c |
|---|---|---|
| 4 + ☐ = 10 | ☐ + 0 = 10 | 9 + ☐ = 10 |
| 5 + ☐ = 10 | ☐ + 5 = 10 | ☐ + 7 = 10 |
| 8 + ☐ = 10 | ☐ + 8 = 10 | 0 + ☐ = 10 |
| 3 + ☐ = 10 | ☐ + 3 = 10 | ☐ + 6 = 10 |

**2** The corner numbers add up to 10. Write the missing corner number.

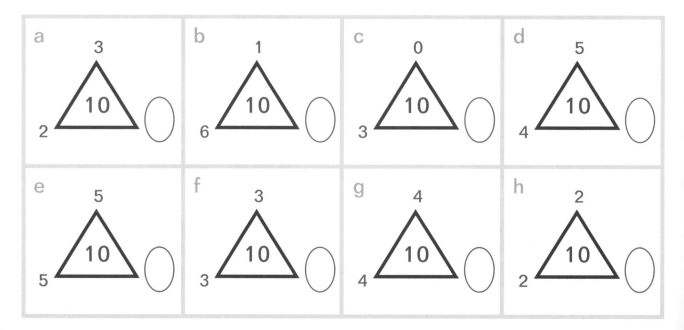

# Unit 6: Subtraction

## Remember

You can count back along a **number line** to help you subtract.

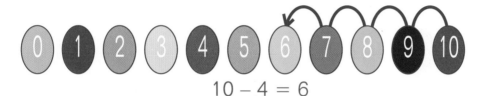

$$10 - 4 = 6$$

## Have a go

1. Write what is being subtracted.

a

$$4 - \boxed{\phantom{0}} = 1$$

b

$$5 - \boxed{\phantom{0}} = 3$$

c

$$10 - \boxed{\phantom{0}} = 6$$

d

$$9 - \boxed{\phantom{0}} = 5$$

2. Write the missing number. Use the number line to help you.

a $\bigcirc - 4 = 2$     b $\bigcirc - 5 = 1$     c $\bigcirc - 3 = 5$

d $\bigcirc - 1 = 9$     e $\bigcirc - 4 = 0$     f $\bigcirc - 7 = 3$

# Unit 7: Subtraction words

## Remember

You can use a **number line** to help you subtract.

0 1 2 3 4 5 6 7 8 9 10

4 less than 8 equals 4

## Have a go

**1** Write in the missing numbers.

| a | b | c |
|---|---|---|
| 3 less than 5 equals ☐ | 3 less than ☐ equals 6 | ☐ less than 4 equals 1 |
| 4 less than 6 equals ☐ | 2 less than ☐ equals 8 | ☐ less than 7 equals 5 |
| 5 less than 7 equals ☐ | 1 less than ☐ equals 8 | ☐ less than 6 equals 5 |
| 3 less than 8 equals ☐ | 4 less than ☐ equals 6 | ☐ less than 5 equals 2 |
| 2 less than 6 equals ☐ | 5 less than ☐ equals 0 | ☐ less than 9 equals 5 |

**2** Answer these number sentences.

a

Subtract 3 from 8 ⬭

b

Take away 5 from 8 ⬭

c

Take 2 from 9 ⬭

d

Count back 3 from 10 ⬭

e

2 subtracted from 5 ⬭

f

10 subtract 7 ⬭

# Unit 8: Finding differences

## Remember

You can count on to find the **difference** between two numbers.

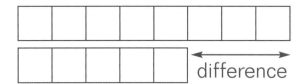

difference

The difference between 5   and   8   is 3.

## Have a go

Use the number line to help you.

1 2 3 4 5 6 7 8 9 10 11 12 13 14 15 16 17 18 19 20

**1** Find the difference between the numbers.

a

4   10

difference = ( )

b

6   8

difference = ( )

c

5   11

difference = ( )

d

9   7

difference = ( )

e

12   5

difference = ( )

f

10   7

difference = ( )

**2** Join up pairs of numbers that have a difference of 2.

4        3        10        5

8        2        9        11

# Unit 9: Money

## Remember

You need to know what these **coins** are worth.

| 1p | 2p | 5p | 10p | 20p | 50p | £1 | £2 |

## Have a go

1. Total these coins.

a  

b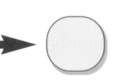

c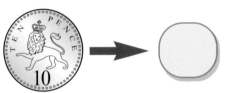

d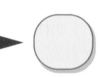

2. How much is in each money bag?

a

b

c

12

## Remember

You can use a **number line** to help you add and subtract.

## Have a go

Finish each number sentence.

a There are 5 fish in a pond.
4 more fish are put in.
There are _____ fish altogether.

b There are 8 cats in a basket.
3 cats run off.
There are _____ cats left.

c There are 10 cherries in a bunch.
6 cherries are eaten.
There are _____ cherries left.

d There are 3 stickers on a page.
3 more stickers are added.
There will be a total of _____ stickers.

e Joe has 3 sweets.
Tom has 2 sweets.
They have _____ sweets altogether.

f Hannah and Will have 10 cards altogether.
Will has 6 cards.
Hannah has _____ cards.

## Remember

A **triangle** is any shape that has **3 straight sides**.

All these are triangles.

## Have a go

1. Join each shape to its name.

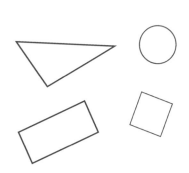

square

triangle

rectangle

circle

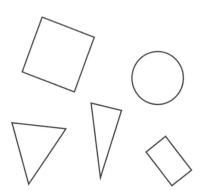

2. There are 5 shapes in each set. Colour the odd one out and write its name.

a

The odd one out is a _____

b

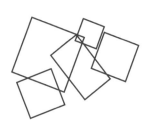

The odd one out is a _____

c

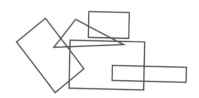

The odd one out is a _____

d

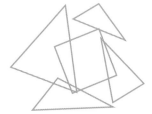

The odd one out is a _____

# Unit 12: Length

We use words like these when measuring.

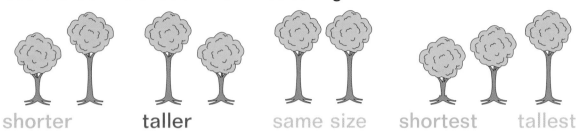

shorter   taller   same size   shortest   tallest

## Have a go

1. Tick all mountains that are taller than the first.

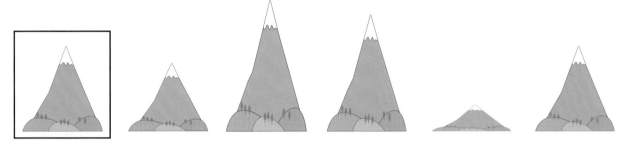

2. Tick all the ladders that are the same size as the first.

3. Tick all the buildings that are shorter than the first.

# Unit 13: Time

## Remember

When the time is 'something' o'clock,

the **minute hand** points to 12.

The **hour hand** shows which o'clock it is.

3 o'clock

## Have a go

Write these o'clock times.

a

b

c

d

e

f

# Unit 14: Pictograms

## Remember

You can use **pictures** to show **information**.

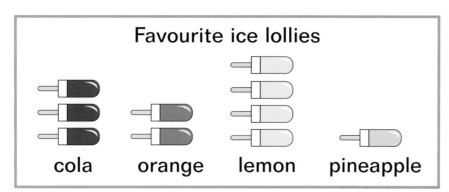

Favourite ice lollies

cola    orange    lemon    pineapple

4 people liked lemon lollies the best.

## Have a go

The graph shows favourite ice creams.

| orange | 🍦🍦🍦🍦🍦 |
|---|---|
| lime | 🍦🍦🍦🍦 |
| mint | 🍦🍦 |
| pineapple | 🍦🍦🍦🍦 |
| vanilla | 🍦🍦🍦🍦🍦🍦 |

a  How many people liked lime the best? _____

b  How many people liked pineapple the best? _____

c  Which ice cream was chosen by 5 people? _____

d  Which ice cream was chosen by 2 people? _____

e  Which ice cream was the most popular? _____

f  Which ice cream was the least popular? _____

Check how much you have learned.

Answer the questions.
Mark your answers. Fill in your score.

**SCORE**

**1** Write the missing numbers.

out of 2

a thirteen = 10 + ☐    b twenty-five = ☐ + 5

**2** Write in the missing numbers.

out of 2

◯ ◯ ◯ ⟨19⟩ ⟨20⟩ ⟨21⟩ ⟨22⟩ ◯ ◯ ◯

**3** Join snakes that are the same length.

out of 3

**4**

a How many cows are there?

**Toy farm animals**

b How many more chickens than horses are there?

out of 2

**5** Write in the two missing numbers.

out of 2

a 3 + ☐ = 10    b ☐ + 8 = 10

6 Use this number line to help you.

0 1 2 3 4 5 6 7 8 9 10

a What is 3 more than 5? __________

b What is the total of 6 and 4? __________

out of 2

7 Join up some dots to make two different triangles.

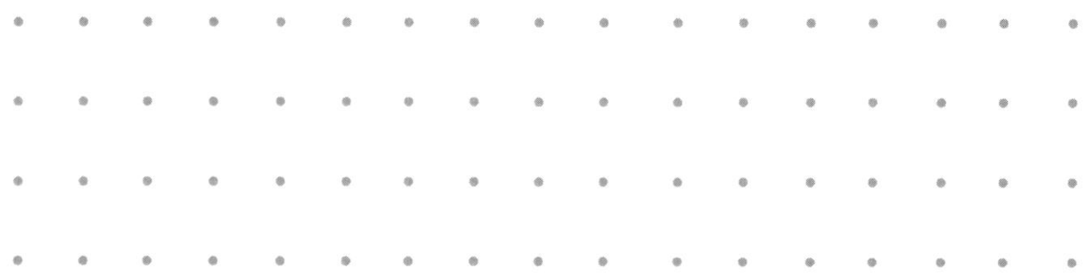

out of 2

8 Write these o'clock times.

a

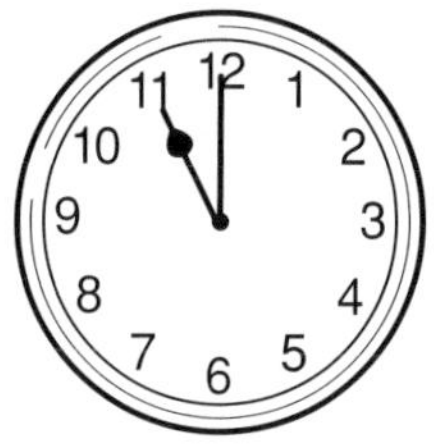

b

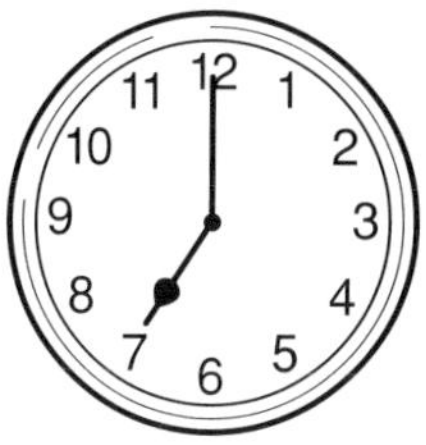

out of 1

0 1 2 3 4 5 6 7 8 9 10

9 Use this number line to help you.

a ( ) – 4 = 6    b 10 – ( ) = 2

out of 2

10 Use the number line to help you.

a Subtract 4 from 10 ( )

b 5 less than ( ) equals 2

out of 2

Total out of 20

# Test 2

Check how much you have learned.

Answer the questions.
Mark your answers. Fill in your score.

**SCORE**

This number line may help you answer some of the questions.

**1** Write in the missing numbers.

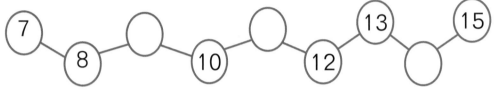

out of 3

**2** This is one rod

out of 1

The ribbon is about _____ rods long.

**3** How many spots are on a double six domino?

a Draw the spots.

b Write the total.

out of 2

**4** Write the difference between these pairs of numbers.

a

difference = ◯

b

difference = ◯

out of 2

**5** Join shapes that match.

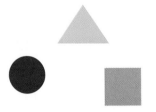  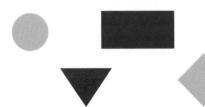 

out of 1

**6** This graph shows favourite types of transport.

| Plane | 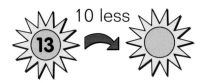 | | | |
|-------|-------|-------|-------|-------|
| Boat |  | | | |

a How many people liked planes the best?

b How many people liked boats the best?

out of 2

**7** Write the missing numbers.

 10 less

 1 more

out of 2

**8** a Colour the bigger number blue.    b Colour the smaller number red.

out of 2

**9** Write the total amounts.

a

b

out of 2

**10** Answer these two problems.

a Tina has 4 pennies. Ben has 9 pennies.
Ben has _____ pennies more than Tina.

out of 2

b Sally has 7 pennies. Vik has 3 pennies.
They have _____ pennies altogether.

Total out of 19

# Parents' notes

**Unit 1: Reading and writing numbers**   Check that your child can say each number from 11 to 20 in words as this can cause problems for some children. How we say the teen numbers is different from numbers that are more than 20 because we say the second number before the first number – 17 is seventeen. With numbers more than 20 we say the first number first – 71 is seventy-one. When you and your child are out and about, encourage him or her to say any numbers up to 100 that you see.

**Unit 2: Comparing numbers**   Your child needs to know that numbers that come after a number are larger, and numbers that come before are smaller. Write the numbers 1 to 20 on small pieces of paper and jumble them up. Choose any pair of numbers that are quite close together such as 11 and 15, and ask your child to find all the numbers that come between these two.

**Unit 3: Addition** All sorts of words are used to mean 'add'. These include 'add', 'total', 'altogether', 'sum' and 'more than'. Your child should be able to answer sums that have words in them as well as the signs. The word for the + sign is 'plus' and for the = sign is 'equals'. It is good practice to give your child 'spoken' sums to answer such as *What is one more than four?*

**Unit 4: Using doubles**   It helps your child's mental addition skills to recognise doubles or near doubles. Eventually your child should remember all the doubles up to double six without having to count the numbers involved. Dice games and domino games will help your child to recognise and quickly total doubles and near doubles.

**Unit 5: Addition facts**   The number pairs that total 10 are particularly important and your child should work hard to start remembering them. Have ten small items on the table. Take turns with your child to cover up some of them with your hand and ask *How many are hiding under my hand?*

**Unit 6: Subtraction**   Your child should recognise the signs – and = and be able to understand how to work out 'missing numbers' in problems such as $4 - \square = 2$ and $\square - 2 = 5$. Making jumps along a number line helps children understand what is happening. For example, – 2 means make two jumps back.

**Unit 7: Subtraction words**   Your child should be able to answer problems that have words in them as well as signs. It is good practice to give your child 'spoken' subtractions to do such as *Subtract two from ten. How many are left?* He or she should know what to do, but may need to use the number line to help work out the answer.

**Unit 8: Finding differences**    One sort of subtraction is called 'difference'. This is not quite the same as 'taking away'. When you find the difference between two numbers, you compare them to see how many more one is than the other. If you count on from the smaller to the larger, this will be the difference.

**Unit 9: Money**    Your child needs to recognise all the coins that we use and to know which is worth the most and which the least. Let your child try to total small sets of two or three coins. Encourage him or her to start with the coin worth most. Being able to count in twos, fives and tens will help.

**Unit 10: Mixed problems**    Your child should be competent in working out addition and subtraction problems using numbers up to 10. At school your child will meet word problems where the addition or subtraction has to be understood through interpreting the words. In this unit your child will be deciding whether to add or subtract in order to solve the problem.

**Unit 11: 2D shapes**    Common 2D shapes that your child should be able to recognise are triangle, circle, square and rectangle. In many books only one type of triangle is shown – the one with three equal sides. In this unit your child will meet all types of triangles and start to know that a triangle is ANY shape that has three straight sides and three corners.

**Unit 12: Length**    Your child needs to compare many different items to find the widest, longest, shortest, tallest and so on. Encourage your child to use a variety of words to describe sizes and not rely just on the words 'big' and 'little'. He or she should also be able to compare one item against others to decide which is longest or shortest. Give your child a pencil and send them on a house hunt to try to find something that is about the same length.

**Unit 13: Time**    Your child should recognise o'clock times on both digital clocks and those with hands. This unit uses clock faces with hands. Talk about o'clock times in 'real time' using a real clock. Use words and phrases such as 'nearly' and 'just past' when talking about o'clock times.

**Unit 14: Pictograms**    Your child should be able to read information from simple picture graphs such as those on page 17. Talk about what each little picture stands for. Ask what their favourite ice cream is and where they would add their choice to the pictogram.

# Answers

## Unit 1: Reading and writing numbers (page 4)

**1**
a 10    b 10    c 10    d 10
e 1    f 3    g 6    h 8
i 20    j 20    k 20    l 20
m 3    n 5    o 6    p 9

**2**

twenty-four → 12
twenty-one → 21
fifteen → 15
fourteen → 14
twenty-five → 25
thirty → 30
twelve → (12)

(12) (21) (30) (25) (15) (14) (24)

## Unit 2: Comparing numbers (page 5)

**1**

14 > 9    13 < 15    17 > 11    18 < 20

**2**

8 > 5    10 < 12    16 > 13    21 > 18

9 > 4    18 > 9    12 < 22    20 > 19

**3**

a (6)→(7)(8)←(9)   b (0)→(1)(2)←(3)

c (10)→(11)(12)←(13)   d (9)→(10)(11)←(12)

e (13)→(14)(15)←(16)   f (17)→(18)(19)←(20)

## Unit 3: Addition (page 6)

**1**
a 8 6 12 11 8    b 3 8 7 7 4
c 2 3 4 3 2

**2**
a 10    b 11    c 7    d 8
e 11    f 7

## Unit 4: Using doubles (page 7)

**1**
a 2    b 8    c 6    d 12
e 10

**2**
a 3    b 9    c 7    d 11
e 5

## Unit 5: Addition facts (page 8)

**1**
a 6 5 2 7    b 10 5 2 7
c 1 3 10 4

**2**
a 5    b 3    c 7    d 1
e 0    f 4    g 2    h 6

## Unit 6: Subtraction (page 9)

**1**
a 3    b 2    c 4    d 4

**2**
a 6    b 6    c 8    d 10
e 4    f 10

## Unit 7: Subtraction words (page 10)

**1**
a 2 2 2 5 4
b 9 10 9 10 5
c 3 2 1 3 4

**2**
a 5    b 3    c 7    d 7
e 3    f 3

## Unit 8: Finding differences (page 11)

**1**
a 6    b 2    c 6
d 2    e 7    f 3

**2**
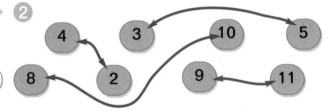

## Unit 9: Money (page 12)

**1**
a 15p    b 20p    c 12p    d 11p

**2**
a 16p    b 15p    c 20p

## Unit 10: Mixed problems (page 13)

**1**
a 9    b 5    c 4    d 6
e 5    f 4

## Unit 11: 2D shapes (page 14)

**1**
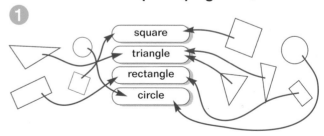

square
triangle
rectangle
circle

## ② a

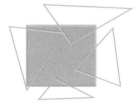

The odd one out is a square.

**b**

The odd one out is a rectangle.

**c**

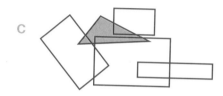

The odd one out is a triangle.

**d**

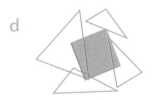

The odd one out is a square.

## Unit 12: Length (page 15)

**1**

**2**

**3**

## Unit 13: Time (page 16)

| a | 1 | b | 5 |
|---|---|---|---|
| c | 10 | d | 6 |
| e | 9 | f | 4 |

## Unit 14: Pictograms (page 17)

| a | 4 | b | 4 | c | orange |
|---|---|---|---|---|---|
| d | mint | e | vanilla | f | mint |

## Test 1 (pages 18 and 19)

**1**  a 3          b 20

**2**  16 17 18          23 24 25

**3**

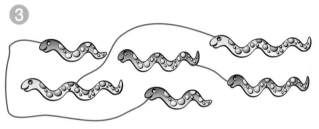

**4**  a 6          b 2

**5**  a 7          b 2

**6**  a 8          b 10

**7**  Check that both shapes are triangles and are different.

**8**  a 11          b 7

**9**  a 10          b 8

**10**  a 6          b 7

## Test 2 (pages 20 and 21)

**1**

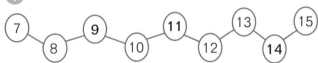

**2**  5

**3**  a

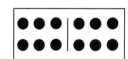

b 12

**4**  a 5          b 8

⑤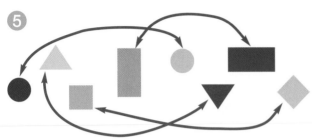

⑥ a  3 people

    b  4 people

⑦ a  3        b  13

⑧ a  **13** **11**

   b  **14** **17**

⑨ a  16p       b  12p

⑩ a  5         b  10

# Unit 1: Making words

## Remember

We can make **words** with **letters**.

m + a + p
map

t + o + p
top

l + i + p
lip

## Have a go

1. Choose **a**, **e**, **i**, **o** or **u** to go in the middle of each word.

| a | b | c | d | e |
|---|---|---|---|---|
| b<u>a</u>t | h__t | w__t | c__t | s__t |
| __bat__ | _____ | _____ | _____ | _____ |

| f | g | h | i | j |
|---|---|---|---|---|
| n__t | h__t | c__t | p__t | d__t |
| _____ | _____ | _____ | _____ | _____ |

2. Write the words with **a** in the middle  _____  _____

3. Write the words with **e** in the middle  _____  _____

4. Write the words with **i** in the middle  _____  _____

5. Write the words with **o** in the middle  _____  _____

6. Write the words with **u** in the middle  _____  _____

 **Remember**

A sentence must **make sense**.
The **words** in a sentence must be in the **right order**.

You cake a eat. ☒          You eat a cake. ☑

 **Have a go**

① Write the words in these sentences in the correct order.
One has been done for you.

a Snow white is.        Snow is white.

b I swim can.          _____

c The hot sun is.       _____

d You book a read.      _____

e A frog hopping likes.  _____

f Some black are cows.   _____

② Match up the sentence beginnings and endings.
Write the sentences you make. One has been done for you.

a A rabbit eats    house.     _____

b I live in a      flowers.    _____

c A lion has four  swim.       _____

d A fish can       carrots. ➤ A rabbit eats carrots.

e Bees like        webs.       _____

f Spiders make     legs.       _____

# Unit 3: Colour words

## Remember

It is helpful to know how to spell colour words.

| | | | | |
|---|---|---|---|---|
| brown | grey | white | yellow | black |
| green | blue | purple | pink | orange |

## Have a go

**1** Write the colour words that begin with:

b _____ _____ _____

g _____ _____

p _____ _____

w _____

y _____

o _____

**2** Write the colour word that rhymes with:

a wink _____          b sack _____

c kite _____          d been _____

e glue _____

**3** Write the colour word that contains the word:

a ran _____          b yell _____

c hit _____          d ink _____

e lack _____

# Unit 4: *Ck* and *ng* at the end of words

## Remember

Some short words end with **ck** and **ng**.

A **duck** says qua**ck**.

You ba**ng** a go**ng**.

## Have a go

**1** Complete these words. One has been done for you.

| ck | | | |
|---|---|---|---|
| sa**ck** | si_____ | so_____ | su_____ |
| <u>sack</u> | _____ | _____ | _____ |

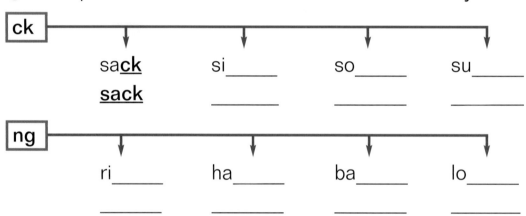

| ng | | | |
|---|---|---|---|
| ri_____ | ha_____ | ba_____ | lo_____ |
| _____ | _____ | _____ | _____ |

**2** Use the words you made in these sentences.

a  You _____ a bell.

b  If you are unwell you feel _____ .

c  You _____ up a picture.

d  You put a _____ on your foot.

e  You _____ a drum.

f  You _____ a sweet.

g  Father Christmas has a _____ of toys.

h  The opposite of short is _____ .

## Remember

Say these words slowly.
Listen to the sound the **first two letters** make.

**cl**ap

**dr**um

## Have a go

1   Choose the correct letters to begin each word.
    One has been done for you.

| a | b | c | d | e |
|---|---|---|---|---|
| tr    cr | pl    cl   pr | pl   fr | fl   cr | cl |
| **tr**ick | __ __ iff | __ __ am | __ __ an | __ __ ack |

| f | g | h | i | j |
|---|---|---|---|---|
| bl    br | cr    dr   cl | gl   fl | fr   pr | pl |
| __ __ ink | __ __ ink | __ __ ass | __ __ og | __ __ ug |

2   Write all the words which have **r** as a second letter.

_____  _____  _____  _____  _____

3   Write all the words which have **l** as a second letter.

_____  _____  _____  _____

# Unit 6: Revising nouns

## Remember

Some words **name** things. They are called **nouns**, or **naming words**.

car

bicycle

lorry

## Have a go

**1** Choose the name of the correct person to complete each sentence.

a A _____ teaches children. (baker/teacher)

b A _____ makes us well. (doctor/vet)

c A _____ looks after our teeth. (driver/dentist)

d A _____ looks after animals. (vet/teacher)

e A _____ drives a lorry. (doctor/driver)

f A _____ bakes bread. (baker/dentist)

**2** Choose the correct noun to complete each sentence.

| shell | sea | nest | burrow | web | stable |
|-------|-----|------|--------|-----|--------|

a A bird lives in a _____.

b A spider lives in a _____.

c A snail lives in a _____.

d A rabbit lives in a _____.

e A horse lives in a _____.

f A fish lives in the _____.

## Remember

When **sh** comes together in a word it makes one sound. It tells you to be quiet – **sh**!

fi**sh**

When **ch** comes together in a word it makes one sound. It sounds like a sneeze – **ch**!

tor**ch**

## Have a go

Write the words here.
Read the words.

① Match up the words that rhyme.

| fish | mesh |
| crash | dish |
| fresh | crush |
| rush | smash |

_____  _____

**fish**  **dish**

_____  _____

_____  _____

② Complete these words with **ch**. Read the words you make.

a  pin**ch**       b  bun_____      c  lun_____      d  clin_____

   **pinch**       _____        _____        _____

e  win_____      f  pun_____      g  fin_____      h  mun_____

   _____        _____        _____        _____

③ Write the **ch** words you made:

| **inch** words | **unch** words |
|---|---|
|  |  |

33

# Unit 8: The *ee* and *ea* sounds

## Remember

The letters **ee** and **ea** often make the **same sound** in words.

You **ea**t a sw**ee**t.

## Have a go

1  Choose **ee** or **ea** to complete each word.
   One has been done for you.

| a | b | c | d |
|---|---|---|---|
| r**ea**d <br> ___**read**___ | b _____ <br> _____ | s ____ t <br> _____ | sw ____ p <br> _____ |

| e | f | g | h |
|---|---|---|---|
| cr ____ p <br> _____ | t ____ ch <br> _____ | l ____ p <br> _____ | p ____ l <br> _____ |

2  Choose **ee** or **ea** to complete each word.
   Read the words you make.

a  f ____ l    b  h ____ p    c  n ____ d    d  w ____ p

e  h ____ t    f  gr ____ n    g  sp ____ k    h  dr ____ m

i  p ____ p    j  n ____ t    k  tr ____

# Unit 9: The *ay* and *ai* sounds

## Remember

The letters **ai** and **ay** often make the **same sound** in words.

rain

bray

| The letters **ai** usually come **within** the word. | The letters **ay** usually come **at the end** of the word. |

## Have a go

Write the words here.

1 Find and ring the **ai** or **ay** words in this puzzle.

```
z a b g h d a y r q
x c v b n a i l y t
r a i n q w e r t y
k j a w a y s x z c
d f g h j p a i n z
p o y h s t a y w ı
d f g t r a y h j c
a i m c v b g t y w
```

___ day ___

_____

_____

_____

_____

_____

_____

_____

2 Choose **ai** or **ay** to complete each word.
  Read the words you make.

| | | | |
| a s_____ | b r_____d | c m_____ | d _____m |
| e pl_____ | f r_____n | g st_____ | h r_____l |
| i cl_____ | j f_____l | k aw_____ | l cl_____m |

## Remember

We begin the names of the **months of the year** with a **capital letter**.

My birthday is in **M**arch.

## Have a go

**1** Rewrite the names of the months of the year in the correct order. Remember to begin each month with a capital letter.

| | | | | | |
|---|---|---|---|---|---|
| february | april | august | january | december | july |
| march | september | june | november | may | october |

_____ _____ _____ _____

_____ _____ _____ _____

_____ _____ _____ _____

**2** Write the names of the months with:

a  3 letters    __ __ __

b  4 letters    __ __ __ __              __ __ __ __

c  5 letters    __ __ __ __ __          __ __ __ __ __

d  6 letters    __ __ __ __ __ __

e  7 letters    __ __ __ __ __ __ __    __ __ __ __ __ __ __

f  8 letters    __ __ __ __ __ __ __ __    __ __ __ __ __ __ __ __

__ __ __ __ __ __ __ __

g  9 letters    __ __ __ __ __ __ __ __ __

## Remember

We ask a **question** when we want to know something.

A question always **begins** with a **capital letter**.

**W**hat are you doing**?**

A question always **ends** with a **question mark**.

## Have a go

Write the questions correctly.
Then write a sensible answer for each question.

a

what is it

_____**What is it?**_____

_____**It is a duck.**_____

b

what can you see

_____

_____

c

what goes fast

_____

_____

d

what goes slowly

_____

_____

e

is it big or small

_____

_____

f

is it round or flat

_____

_____

g

where is the boy

_____

_____

h

where is the girl

_____

_____

## Remember

Some words tell us what people or things **do**.
They are called **verbs**, or **doing words**.

running

swimming

## Have a go

**1**  Make some doing words. One has been done for you.

a  brush + ing = <u>**brushing**</u>      b  cook + ing = _____

c  crawl + ing = _____      d  jump + ing = _____

e  catch + ing = _____      f  cry + ing = _____

g  draw + ing = _____      h  laugh + ing = _____

**2**  Use the doing words you made.
Write each doing word under the correct picture.

## Remember

The letters **oa** and **ow** often make the **same sound** in words.

boat

crow

> The letters **oa** usually come **within** the word.

> The letters **ow** often come at the **end** of the word.

## Have a go

1　Choose **oa** or **ow** to complete each word.
One has been done for you.

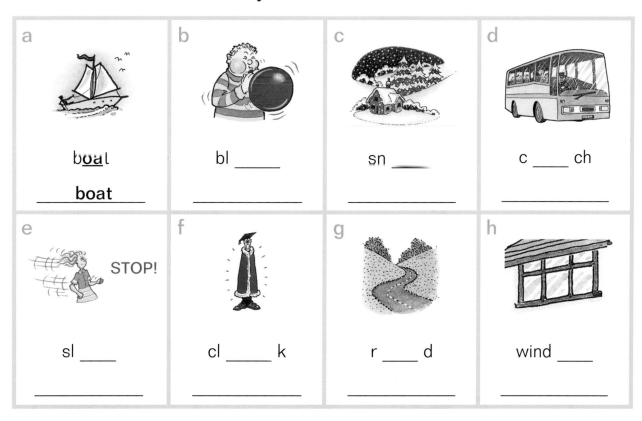

| a | b | c | d |
|---|---|---|---|
| b<u>oa</u>t <br> ___ **boat** ___ | bl _____ <br> _____ | sn _____ <br> _____ | c _____ ch <br> _____ |
| e STOP! <br> sl _____ <br> _____ | f <br> cl _____ k <br> _____ | g <br> r _____ d <br> _____ | h <br> wind _____ <br> _____ |

2　Choose **oa** or **ow** to complete each word. Read the words you make.

a b____st   b l____   c t____   d s___k   e f____m   f cr____

g l___d   h yell____   i s___p   j g___l   k arr____

## Remember

Listen to the sound of the **u** in these words:

cub           cube

The magic **e** at the end of **cube** makes the **u** say its name.

## Have a go

**1** Make some new words. Read the new words you make.

a pip + e = __pipe__     b mad + e = _____     c cod + e = _____

d tap + e = _____     e slim + e = _____     f not + e = _____

g us + e = _____     h rod + e = _____     i tub + e = _____

**2** Choose the correct word.

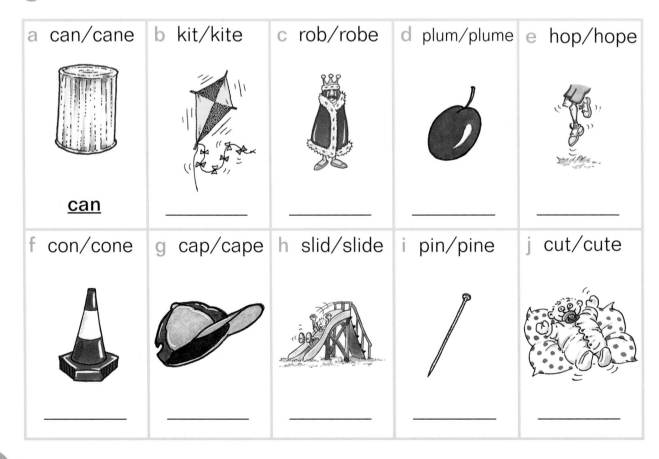

| a can/cane | b kit/kite | c rob/robe | d plum/plume | e hop/hope |
|---|---|---|---|---|
| __can__ | _____ | _____ | _____ | _____ |
| f con/cone | g cap/cape | h slid/slide | i pin/pine | j cut/cute |
| _____ | _____ | _____ | _____ | _____ |

# Test 1

Check how much you have learned.

Answer the questions.
Mark your answers. Fill in your score.

**1** Choose the correct letter to complete each word.

a
b     f

__ox

b
h     t

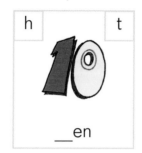

__en

out of 2

**2** Write the words in each sentence in the correct order.

a   like   sweets.   I   eating

_____

b   is   sun   hot.   The

_____

out of 2

**3** Write the correct colour word in each sentence.

a   A banana is _____.

b   Grass is _____.

out of 2

**4** Choose the correct word for each gap.

a   I feel _____ (sack, sick).

b   I read a _____ (long, lung) story.

out of 2

**5** What is it?

a
frog or flog?

_____

b
prank or plank?

_____

out of 2

Total out of 10

# Test 2

Check how much you have learned.

Answer the questions.
Mark your answers. Fill in your score.

**1** Choose the correct naming word for each gap.

a  A spider lives in a _____ (nest, web).

b  A _____ (teacher, baker) makes bread.

out of 2

**2** Choose **ch** or **sh** to complete the words.

a           b

a bun___ of bananas          a di___ of soup

out of 2

**3** Choose the correct word for each gap.

a  You _____ (reed, read) a book.

b  You _____ (peel, peal) an orange.

out of 2

**4** Choose **ai** or **ay** to complete the words.

a 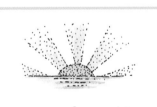          b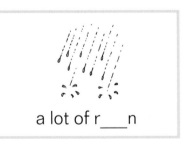

a r___ of sunshine          a lot of r___n

out of 2

**5** Answer these questions:

a What is the month after April?

_____

b What is the month before December?

_____

out of 2

**6** Write this question correctly. Answer **yes** or **no**.

is a red flag blue

_____ _____

out of 2

**7** Write the correct doing word under each picture.

running

diving

a

b

_____ _____

out of 2

**8** Complete the missing words.

a In football you can score a g_____.

b Each year you g_____ taller.

out of 2

**9** Choose the correct word to fill each gap.

a You fly a _____ (kit, kite).

b You _____ (cut, cute) with a knife.

out of 2

Total out of 18

# Parents' notes

**Unit 1: Making words**  Knowing the sounds of individual letters and being able to blend them together to build simple words is an important early step in reading and writing.

**Unit 2: Writing sensible sentences**  Most texts are written in sentences. A sentence is a meaningful unit which makes sense on its own. The order in which words are arranged is of vital importance in being able to make sense of what has been written.

**Unit 3: Colour words**  There are many words which occur frequently in reading, which your child needs to be familiar with. Sometimes these may be grouped together in topics, such as 'colour words'.

**Unit 4: *Ck* and *ng* at the end of words**  It is uncommon to find short words ending in 'c' – such words usually end with **ck**. Another common word ending is **ng**. Remind your child that these letters make one sound when they occur together.

**Unit 5: Revising initial letter blends**  Many words begin with two consonants e.g. **cl**, **pr**, **st**. Help your child to sound out both consonants and blend them together.

**Unit 6: Revising nouns**  All words may be classified according to the jobs they do in sentences. Naming words (or nouns) play an essential part in grammar.

**Unit 7: Words with *ch* and *sh***  Sometimes when two letters come together they make just one sound e.g. **ch** and **sh**. It may be helpful for your child to remember that **ch** is the sneezing sound (ch!) whilst **sh** is the quiet sound (sh!).

**Unit 8: The *ee* and *ea* sounds**  All words are made up of phonemes (units of sound). Sometimes phonemes may be single letters. Sometimes they consist of two or more letters which make one sound e.g. **ee** and **ea**. Remind your child that both these phonemes make the same sound in the words studied.

**Unit 9: The *ay* and *ai* sounds**  The phonemes **ay** and **ai** both make the same sound in words. One good tip to remember is that **ai** usually comes within a word, whereas **ay** usually comes at the end of a word.

**Unit 10: The months of the year**  Remind your child that we use capital letters to begin sentences but we also use them at the beginning of the names of the months of the year.

**Unit 11: Questions and answers**   We ask questions when we want to find something out. A question is a type of sentence. It should begin with a capital letter and always end with a question mark.

**Unit 12: Revising verbs**   All words may be classified according to the jobs they do in sentences. Doing words (or verbs) play an essential part in grammar.

**Unit 13: The *oa* and *ow* sounds**   The phonemes **oa** and **ow** both make the same sound in words in this unit. One good tip to remember is that **oa** always comes within a word, whereas **ow** often comes at the end of a word.

**Unit 14: Using magic *e* in words**   The **e** at the end of some short words is often called 'magic' because of the way it affects the vowel in the middle of the word e.g. hat – hate. It has the effect of changing the middle vowel from a short sound (as in mat) to a long sound (as in pay).

# Answers

## Unit 1: Making words (page 27)
**1** a b<u>a</u>t  b h<u>o</u>t  c w<u>e</u>t  d c<u>u</u>t  e s<u>i</u>t
  f n<u>e</u>t  g h<u>u</u>t  h c<u>a</u>t  i p<u>i</u>t  j d<u>o</u>t

**2** bat  cat

**3** wet  net

**4** sit  pit

**5** hot  dot

**6** cut  hut

## Unit 2: Writing sensible sentences (page 28)
**1** a  Snow is white.
  b  I can swim.
  c  The sun is hot.
  d  You read a book.
  e  A frog likes hopping.
  f  Some cows are black.

**2** I live in a house.
  Bees like flowers.
  A fish can swim.
  A rabbit eats carrots.
  Spiders make webs.
  A lion has four legs.

## Unit 3: Colour words (page 29)
**1** b blue  black  brown
  g grey  green
  p pink  purple
  w white
  y yellow
  o orange

**2** a pink  b black  c white
  d green  e blue

**3** a <u>o</u>range  b <u>yell</u>ow  c w<u>hite</u>
  d p<u>i</u>nk  e b<u>lack</u>

## Unit 4: *Ck* and *ng* at the end of words (page 30)
**1** sack  sick  sock  suck
  ring  hang  bang  long

**2** a ring  b sick  c hang  d sock
  e bang  f suck  g sack  h long

## Unit 5: Revising initial letter blends (page 31)
**1** a trick  b cliff  c pram  d flan
  e crack  f blink  g drink  h glass
  i frog  j plug

**2** trick  pram  crack  drink  frog

**3** cliff  flan  blink  glass  plug

## Unit 6: Revising nouns (page 32)
**1** a teacher  b doctor  c dentist
  d vet  e driver  f baker

**2** a nest  b web  c shell
  d burrow  e stable  f sea

## Unit 7: Words with *ch* and *sh* (page 33)
**1** fresh  mesh
  fish  dish
  rush  crush
  crash  smash

**2** a pinch  b bunch  c lunch
  d clinch  e winch  f punch
  g finch  h munch

**3**

| inch | | unch | |
|------|------|------|------|
| pinch | winch | bunch | punch |
| clinch | finch | lunch | munch |

## Unit 8: The *ee* and *ea* sounds (page 34)
**1** a read  b bee  c seat  d sweep
  e creep  f teach  g leap  h peel

**2** a feel  b heap  c need  d weep
  e heat  f green  g speak  h dream
  i peep  j neat  k tree

## Unit 9: The *ay* and *ai* sounds (page 35)

**1**

```
z a b g h (d a y) r q       ___ day
x c v b (n a i l) y t       ___ nail
(r a i n) q w e r t y       ___ rain
k j (a w a y) s x z c       ___ away
d f g h j (p a i n) z       ___ pain
p o y h (s t a y) w r       ___ stay
d f g (t r a y) h j c       ___ tray
(a i m) c v b g t y w       ___ aim
```

**2**  a  say    b  raid    c  may    d  aim
e  play    f  rain    g  stay    h  rail
i  clay    j  fail    k  away    l  claim

## Unit 10: The months of the year (page 36)

**1**  January   February   March
April   May   June   July
August   September   October
November   December

**2**  a  May    b  June July
c  March April    d  August
e  January October
f  February November December
g  September

## Unit 11: Questions and answers (page 37)

Other answers are possible.
a  What is it?    It is a duck.
b  What can you see?    I can see a boy.
c  What goes fast?    A car goes fast.
d  What goes slowly?    A snail goes slowly.
e  Is it big or small?    It is big.
f  Is it round or flat?    It is round.
g  Where is the boy?    The boy is in bed.
h  Where is the girl?    The girl is on a bike.

## Unit 12: Revising verbs (page 38)

**1**  a  brushing  b  cooking  c  crawling
d  jumping  e  catching  f  crying
g  drawing  h  laughing

**2**  a  crawling  b  drawing  c  jumping
d  brushing  e  laughing  f  cooking
g  catching  h  crying

## Unit 13: The *oa* and *ow* sounds (page 39)

**1**  a  boat  b  blow  c  snow  d  coach
e  slow  f  cloak g  road  h  window

**2**  a  boast  b  low    c  tow    d  soak
e  foam  f  crow  g  load  h  yellow
i  soap  j  goal  k  arrow

## Unit 14: Using magic *e* in words (page 40)

**1**  a  pipe    b  made  c  code  d  tape
e  slime  f  note    g  use    h  rode
i  tube

**2**  a  can    b  kite    c  robe  d  plum
e  hop    f  cone    g  cap    h  slide
i  pin    j  cute

## Test 1 (page 41)

**1**  a  fox              b  ten

**2**  a  I like eating sweets.
b  The sun is hot.

**3**  a  A banana is yellow.
b  Grass is green.

**4**  a  sick              b  long

**5**  a  frog              b  plank

**Test 2 (pages 42 and 43)**

**1**  a  A spider lives in a <u>web</u>.
    b  A <u>baker</u> makes bread.

**2**  a  a bun<u>ch</u> of bananas
    b  a di<u>sh</u> of soup

**3**  a  You <u>read</u> a book.
    b  You <u>peel</u> an orange.

**4**  a  ray         b  rain

**5**  a  May        b  November

**6**  Is a red flag blue?   No.

**7**  a  diving      b  running

**8**  a  goal        b  grow

**9**  a  kite        b  cut